Introducing Macramé

INTRODUCING MACRAMÉ

Eirian Short

B T BATSFORD LIMITED   LONDON
WATSON-GUPTILL PUBLICATIONS   NEW YORK

B T Batsford Limited
4 Fitzhardinge Street, London, W 1 and
Watson-Guptill Publications
165 West 46th Street, New York, NY 10036

Contents

Acknowledgment

I should like to thank the British Museum, the National Maritime Museum and the Embroiderers' Guild for permission to reproduce work from their collections. Also the following private collectors who kindly lent historical and modern examples: Mrs Valerie Cliffe, Miss Dorothy Holman, Miss Ann Mary Pilcher, Mrs Greta Raikes, Miss Janet Rider and Miss Marianne Straub.

My thanks to Miss A K Davies, Principal of Wall Hall College of Education, Mr J C Downing, Principal of Stourbridge College of Art, Mr H H Shelton, Principal of Hornsey College of Art, and Mrs Valerie Cliffe, Head of the Fashion and Textiles department at Bath College of Home Economics, for permission to use work done by their students.

The following people have lent work or photographs of work and to them also I am very grateful: Miss Ann Croot, Miss Ellyn Elson, Mrs Marion Smith Ferri, Miss Margaret Gains, Mr Michael Halsey, Miss Elaine Henning, Miss Althea Hill, Mrs Cassandra Mayne, Miss Janet Oliver, Miss Carol Outram, Mr George Pfiffner, Miss Jane Smith, Mrs Sheila Sharp, Miss Judith Stone and Joanna Thomas.

My grateful thanks to my husband, Denys Short, who took all but a few of the photographs and helped in so many other ways, and to all the people who gave advice, made suggestions and tracked down historical examples.

ES
London 1970

Introduction

Just as appliqué evolved from the utilitarian patch, so a number of different styles of decorative knotting have developed from the simple process of tying two threads together. One of these is macramé, and the fact that it is such a basic method, needing no tools but the fingers, makes macramé particularly satisfying to work. Outlay on equipment is minimal, and, although there *are* mechanical aids to facilitate the work, it is possible to produce varied and interesting work with virtually no equipment at all.

With the two main basic knots, the flat (or reef) knot and the half hitch, patterns of infinite variety can be created. Some other knots are explained but these are an embellishment to macramé rather than an essential. The wide braid in figure 77, for example, is worked entirely with flat knots and half hitches.

Macramé can be made into braids and fringes which, depending on the type of thread used, are suitable for decorating clothes, accessories or household articles. Made up into a fabric, it can be strong and hardwearing and makes excellent curtains, screens, bags, coats, jackets, etc. In the past it has been mainly confined to useful articles, decorative though these might incidentally be, but at present it is being used as a medium for wall-hangings, panels and 'sculpture'. In this context it may be used alone or combined with fabric collage, embroidery or three-dimensional construction.

Whatever category of work is planned, threads are worked in one continuous length, so that, once the knotting threads are attached, there are no interruptions and work grows quickly under the fingers.

No 'recipes' are given in the book, for, once the knots are learned and understood, it is a simple matter to

1 Detail from an Assyrian frieze (circa 850 BC) showing a heavily fringed military tunic *By courtesy of the Trustees of the British Museum*

'read' a pattern from a photograph or drawing. It is hoped, however, that the work shown here will not be copied, but will act as a starting point for ideas, and that the reader, having grasped the principles of macramé will go on to create original and exciting designs.

The history of Macramé

Knots play an important part in the lives of primitive people, being used in fishing, hunting, the trapping of wild animals and the harnessing of tame ones; for securing canoes, rafts and huts; and also for dress. The knotting together of vines, withes, grasses, sinews and leather thongs must have been one of the earliest craft forms, preceding even the simplest weaving. Even in our sophisticated society knots are still used by most people in their domestic life or their trade or profession. The housewife, the nurse, the surgeon, the sailor, the mountaineer, the butcher and the angler all have their own particular repertoire of knots.

Even the most utilitarian of processes soon develops a decorative side. The decorative work may still retain the original useful function, or the decoration may become an end in itself. Decorative knotting has branched out into several distinct forms and has also served as a basis for designs in other media, such as stone carving, bookbinding and illuminating.

Each different branch of decorative knotting has developed its own characteristics; sailors' 'fancy knotting', for instance, being quite unlike macramé, although both forms are sometimes combined in one piece of work. Macramé probably originated in the Middle East, where as long ago as the ninth century BC warriors wore garments edged with heavy plaited or knotted fringes (figure 1).

In the Arab world, the work took on a similar surface quality to the architecture with its abstract all-over pattern, geometric in character and rich in texture. From the Arab countries macramé spread northwards into Europe, being taken to Italy by the returning crusaders and to Spain by the Moors.

9

2 Two figures, one male, one female, from a piece of sixteenth century Italian macramé lace

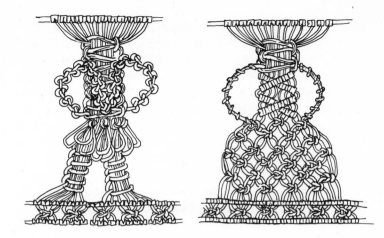

When a weaver removes a finished piece of work from the loom there are, at either end, lengths of spare warp threads and it was a natural development for the weaver, instead of cutting off these ends, to knot them into a decorative fringe. This kind of work was necessarily

3 Victorian edging in coarse twine
Loaned by Janet Rider

fine in character, and evolved simultaneously with other forms of early bobbin and needlepoint lace. It was usually known as *Punto Gropo* or *Groposi* (knotted point), but also sometimes referred to as *Arabeschi* or *Moreschi*, obvious references to its place of origin. Figure 2 shows two formalized figures, one male, one female, from the lace on a sixteenth century Italian cloth. The word macramé did not come into use until the middle of the nineteenth century and appears to come from the Turkish word *Makrama*, meaning a fringed napkin or kerchief, or the arab word *Migramah*, an embroidered veil. Later the word came to be applied to the fringing itself and eventually to any work of this kind. During the sixteenth century *Punto Gropo* was mainly confined to fringes and inset strips on cloths and borders on ecclesiastical vestments. There is in the Louvre a painting by Paul Veronese (1528–1588) called the *Repast of Simon the Pharisee*, which has, in the foreground, a cloth with a deep macramé border.

Eventually macramé spread northwards and is reputed to have been brought to England by Mary, wife of William of Orange, when she left Holland to live in England. The work, which was by now coarser in character, became popular as a pastime in Court circles, and was particularly suitable for work in the evenings when poor light made fine work difficult. There is an account of Queen Charlotte, wife of George III owning frames for knotting, and it appears to have remained in vogue throughout the eighteenth century and into the nineteenth century.

There was also some very fine work being done in the eighteenth century. The Victoria and Albert Museum has a magnificent sampler, whether of English

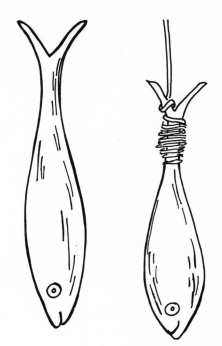

4 Carved bone fish used as bobbins for fine macramé thread. Later, when work became coarser, the fish were often used as game counters, being very like the ones made for that purpose . *From the collection of Greta Raikes*

5 Eighteenth century reticule worked in fine criss-cross bars of flat knots and lined with silk *From the collection of Ann Mary Pilcher*

6 *Left* Small bag knotted in fine white twine *From the collection of Ann Mary Pilcher*

7 *Right* Victorian reticule, the lower half in macramé, the upper half in red silk *From the collection of Greta Raikes*

or Italian origin is unknown, consisting of about eighty small pieces of macramé sewn on to a linen square. They are mostly extremely fine braids in multi-coloured silks and metal threads. One piece, in what is now known as Cavandoli work, has letters and the date 1749 incorporated into it. The sampler is not on show at the Museum but can be seen on request.

Interest in macramé seems to have been maintained in the Mediterranean area, and in the middle of the nineteenth century macramé was being taught to boys and girls in schools and convents along the Riviera and at Genoa. These young pupils soon became proficient enough to produce work which could be sold. As well as

selling on the home market, much of it was exported to South America and California. The work was also spreading to the Americas by other routes. The Spaniards had introduced it into Mexico where it became very popular, giving rise to the name Mexican lace as an alternative to macramé. The east coast Indians of Canada learnt the art from French sailors and made macramé belts, garters and bands, using a variety of 'threads'. Among these were cedar bark, basswood fibre, deer sinew, grass string and 'babiche' (rawhide). The Indians of Quebec made long sashes in a mixture of weaving and knotting with the fingers, which they used as trading items. Some Indian tribes even made robes from rabbit skins rolled and knotted, the knots being worked close together so that the fur covered the holes between the knots.

Sailors were responsible for carrying macramé to many parts of the world. Decorative knotting of all kinds had been done at sea from the days of galleys, when, unless there was some crisis on hand, half the watch rowed while the other half rested. During this leisure time they occupied themselves with making carved and knotted articles which they sold when they came into port. This kind of trade or barter was probably the way macramé was introduced to the Far Eastern countries.

Although the term macramé is used in nautical circles, the work is more often referred to as 'square knotting' and sometimes as 'McNamara's lace'.

Although done by all seamen, macramé was more popular in the Royal Navy where quarters were cramped and larger work difficult. Macramé could be carried out in fishing line and fine twines, and was made into a

8 Ornate Victorian Collar in fine macramé, with bead and tassel decorations. The collar is quite large, the single tassel hanging down the back, the other two forming revers in the front *From the collection of Greta Raikes*

13

9 Part of a nineteenth century Chinese over-skirt made in strips, each strip embroidered, and two with macramé fringes. The knotting is in multi-coloured silks with minute Turks' heads on the tassels *By courtesy of the Embroiderers' Guild*

variety of articles to decorate the ship. Fringes were made for sea chest covers, tablecloths, binnacle, capstan wheel and bell covers. Bell ropes were knotted and spray screens made for launches; even eyescreens were made for accommodation ladders used by women, to hide their legs from view as they went down them.

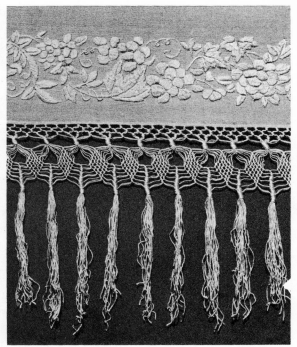

In mid-nineteenth century England macramé came into its own with the fashion for florid, overdecorated interiors. It was used in the drawing room for fringes on mantelpieces, shelves, brackets and tablecovers, and in the bedroom for watch pockets, hair tidies and pincushions. It remained popular throughout the century

10   *Left*   Set of Victorian 'tidies' in white string, lined with red silk *Loaned by Ann Mary Pilcher*

11   *Right*   Fascinator in shantung, with white silk embroidery and knotted fringe. The latter is carried out entirely in overhand knots   *By courtesy of the Embroiderers' Guild*

15

and into the Edwardian era, being used also as dress decoration and for accessories. Many of the pattern books from this time are in German and French, one of the finest being by Thérèse de Dillmont, author of the famous *Encyclopaedia of Needlework*. It is possible to find old pattern books in secondhand bookshops, and although many are in foreign languages the patterns are quite easily 'read' and can be followed without any recourse to the text. The *Encyclopaedia of Needlework*, which has an excellent chapter on macramé, has just been re-issued in facsimile (see *Bibliography*, page 92).

Articles on macramé have appeared sporadically in magazines and books throughout the twentieth century, but it is only in recent years that it has begun to be used really creatively as an art medium. Now, on both sides of the Atlantic, it is being used both in two dimensional hangings and in 'sculptures' and constructions in the round. There is also much commercially produced work in the shops, in the form of shopping bags, handbags, etc of quite a good standard of design and craftmanship. These come from as far afield as the Mediterranean countries and Communist China.

Plate 1   Opposite
Mexican Sun by Eirian Short. The design was started in the centre by setting threads on to a small curtain ring. New threads were set on where necessary

16

Throughout this book the word 'thread' is used to describe the knotting agent, regardless of its composition. Most of the threads suggested for use are readily available from stationers, garden suppliers, hardware stores, needlecraft shops, but a list of specialist suppliers in Great Britain is given on page 90.

As the basis of macramé is the knot, it is obviously essential that the thread used should be strong and easy to handle, and that it should keep its shape when tied. Generally speaking, firm twisted threads are best, although plastic covered twines and tubular synthetic yarns can be used quite successfully.

Materials

12   Solomon's Bar with picots worked in different thicknesses of thread. *From left to right*   Sisal, piping cord No 3, rug wool, piping cord No 00, fine twine, plastic covered twine, crochet cotton No 3

When selecting a suitable thread for a particular purpose, the following points should be kept in mind.

(*a*) The scale of the work. For instance, whereas crochet cotton would be ideal for a braid on a child's dress, a floor rug would demand a thick rug wool or sisal (also known as sisal hemp).

(*b*) Wearing qualities. Parcel string or nylon twine would be more suitable for a belt than wool, which would eventually wear with constant passing through the buckle; similarly, an everyday handbag needs a tougher thread than an evening bag which has only occasional use.

(*c*) Colour range available. Knitting wools, rug wools and embroidery threads offer the widest colour ranges. Nylon twines come in very bright, clear colours, but in a limited range. Piping cord, string vest cotton, which normally only come in white, can be dyed successfully at home, though care must be taken to avoid streaky results. The best way is to wind the thread into skeins and tie loosely in several places with sewing cotton (figure 14). If a big enough container is used, and the skeins kept moving gently, the results should be perfect. Many of the threads used for work in this book have been treated in this way.

13   Sampler in crochet cotton No 10 worked by Hilda Roe, a student at Well Hall College of Education

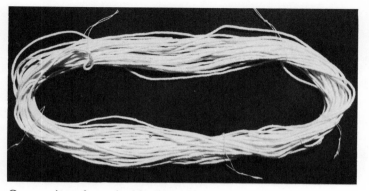

14   Skein of piping cord loosely tied with sewing cotton in preparation for dyeing

Suggestions for suitable threads

Parcels strings and twines of all descriptions.

Nylon and plastic covered twines.

String vest cotton, dishcloth cotton.

Piping cord, available very cheaply in boxes of twenty-five to three hundred yards, depending on the thickness.

Rug wool, knitting wools.

Crochet cotton, embroidery cottons such as pearl and soft (stranded is not suitable). Embroidery cottons have the disadvantage of working out very expensively in the quantities required for knotting, although the colour range is wide.

Tubular synthetic cord.

Rouleau strips made from fabric cut on the bias. This is only feasible where fairly short lengths are needed.

Synthetic metal threads.

Paper rope, as used in theatrical work. This is obviously not suitable for utilitarian articles, but can be used for hangings and panels.

Cellophane string.

Raffia is not ideal, being too flat to knot successfully, but can be worked in with other, more rounded threads.

Equipment

No special equipment is absolutely essential to the working of macramé. The foundation thread to which the knotting threads (warp threads) are fixed should be kept taut and this can be done in a number of ways. Suggestions given on these pages are, by pinning with strong drawing pins to the working table or a board (figure 15); by tying to the posts of an upright chair (figure 16) or by wedging the ends into tightly shut adjacent drawers (figure 17).

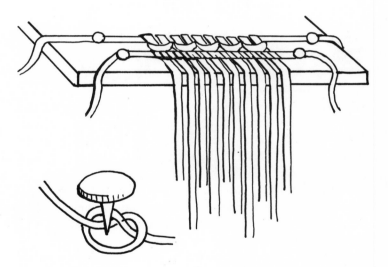

15   Foundation cords attached with drawing pins to board or table

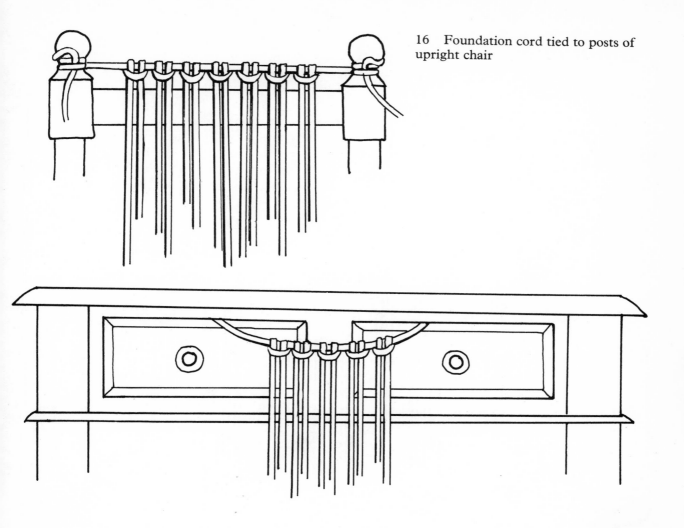

16 Foundation cord tied to posts of upright chair

17 The ends of the foundation cord tucked into tightly shut drawers

A slightly more elaborate way is to fix two G-clamps to the table and suspend the foundation thread between them. These clamps can also be used, spaced at the required distance, for measuring out warps. The clamps which hold the net on a table tennis set make a good substitute if G-clamps are not available.

A piece of soft board is useful when carrying around small pieces of macramé to work. It has the added advantage that pins can be stuck in where needed to keep the work in shape (figure 19). A bulldog clip will hold the work firmly at the top.

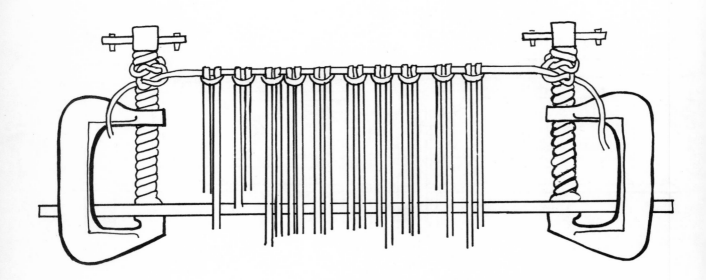

18　Cord suspended between G-clamps, which are screwed to the table

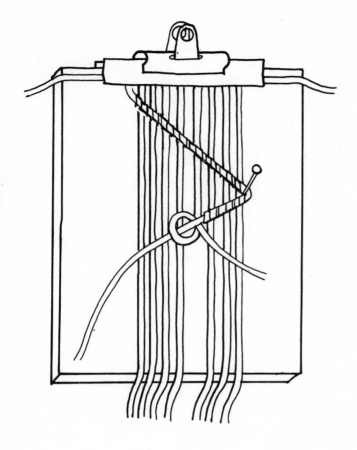

In the past there have been many elaborate macramé desks and frames on the market. A fairly simple one which could be easily copied is shown in figure 20, with the original piece of work on it, unfinished. It consists of a

20 Piece of Victorian knotting
in situ on a macramé desk

flat board with wooden battens fixed to either end to
raise the work slightly. In these strips are drilled holes
to take wooden nails or pegs in a variety of positions, to
which the foundation cords can be tied. On the back are
two hinged flaps which, when out, support the desk at
a comfortable angle for working, but which fold flat
for storage (figure 21).

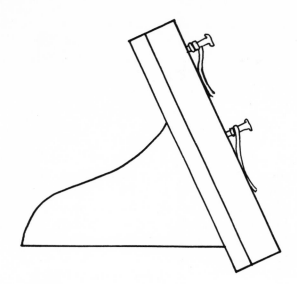

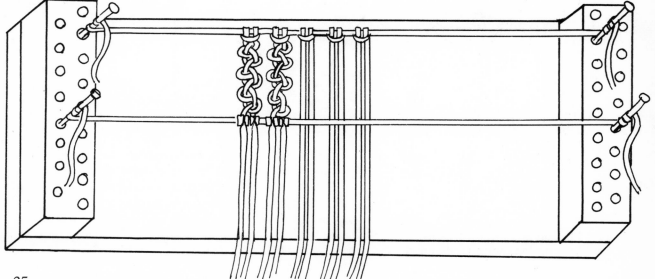

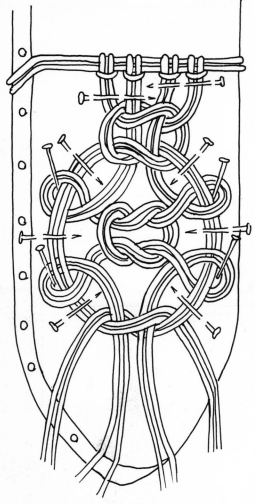

Another easily-made traditional aid to work is a heavy pillow. This can be filled with sand which is heavy enough in itself, or with bran or sawdust, in which case it will have to be weighted. The pillow in figure 24 is filled with sawdust and has inside a 2 lb iron weight from a pair of scales. This stops the pillow moving about during work. Alternatively, rubber suckers could be attached underneath the pillow to grip the table.

Where knots have to be pinned out flat (eg, josephine knots or japanese knots), the top of an ironing table makes a convenient working surface (figure 22).

Other items which come in useful for macramé work are crochet hooks, for setting threads directly into fabric (figure 25) and for getting at awkwardly placed threads; rug and tapestry needles, for finishing off ends, threading beads etc; rubber bands for securing bundles of long warp threads; and milliner's pins or glass headed pins for holding the work in place during progress.

22   The top of an ironing board
used for pinning out intricate knots

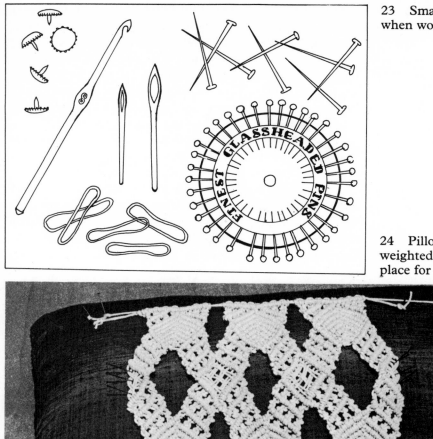

23 Small items which are useful when working macramé

24 Pillow stuffed with sawdust and weighted, with macramé pinned in place for working

Setting on threads

The warp threads must be knotted directly on to fabric (figure 25) or on to a foundation thread (figure 26). This is known as *setting on*. If the macramé is to be worked from the ends of the fabric, no setting on is required (figure 61). As the warp threads are always set on double, the simplest method is to pull the looped end through the fabric or over the foundation thread from front to back and pull the free ends through the loop (figures 25 and 26).

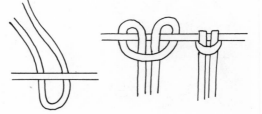

25 Setting on directly to fabric

26 Simple method of setting on over foundation cord

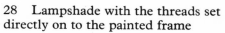

27 Weavers' knot, used for joining on a new warp thread when necessary.

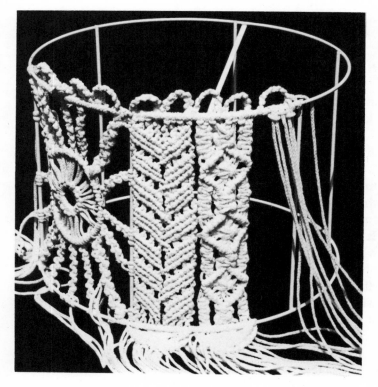

28 Lampshade with the threads set directly on to the painted frame

When a more decorative heading is needed, the setting on may be done more elaborately, using picots or scallops. Picots need to be worked on a pillow or soft board as pins have to be inserted during the working. Scalloped headings can be worked on any taut foundation thread.

The headings which are shown opposite are worked as follows:

Left (figures 29a, 30–32)

Above   Overhand knots

Centre   Chains

Below   Loops and flat knots

Right (figures 29b, 33–35)

Above   Scallops of half-hitches

Centre   Scallops of chains

Below   Simple loops

In each case, a row of cording is worked immediately after the picots or scallops to secure them. Once this is done, the pins may be removed from the picots.

Detailed diagrams of the working of these headings are shown on pages 32 and 33.

Cut the threads eight times the required length of the finished article, ie four times when doubled. For very thick threads such as sisal, allow more, up to twelve times (six times when doubled). Never skimp on thread. It is neither easy nor very satisfactory to join threads while work is in progress. If a thread *does* run out, a new one can be attached by means of a weavers' knot (figure 27). This should be pulled very tight, the ends trimmed and the knot hidden on the back of the work. It is not recommended to join threads unless absolutely necessary.

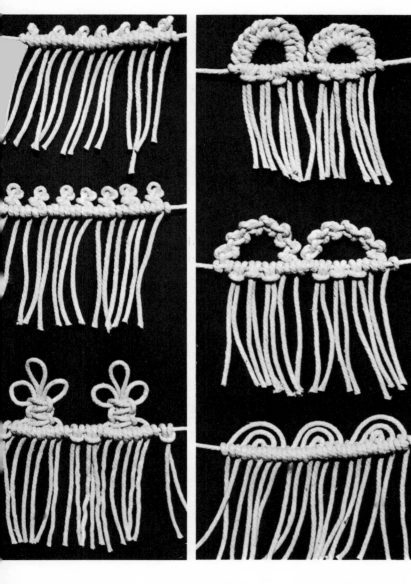

29a *Above* Overhand knots and cording
Centre Chains and cording
Below Picots, flat knots and cording

29b *Above* Scallops of half-hitches
Centre Scallops of chains
Below Simple loops and cording

30 Overhand knots and cording

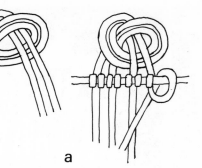

a

31 Chains and cording

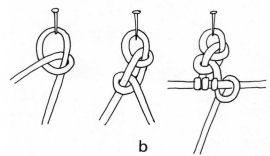

b

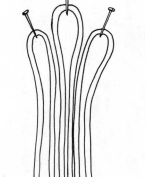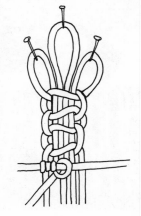

32 Picots, flat knots and cording

c

Plate 2
Hanging by Carol Outram.
Approximately 1525 mm (5 ft) long,
worked in wool with beads

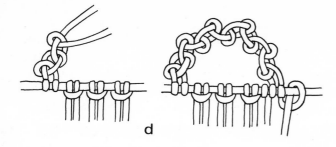

d

33   Scallops of half-hitches

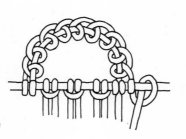

e

34   Scallops of chains

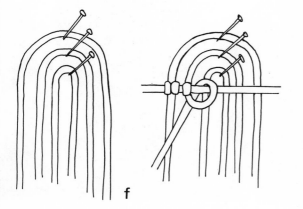

f

35   Simple loops and cording

33

The knots

Macramé is worked almost entirely from two knots with their variations. The first of these is the *simple knot* (figure 36a and b) and it will be seen that it is, in fact, the same as a blanket stitch, or the knot known to sailors and Boy Scouts as the *half-hitch*. The term *half-hitch* is used generally in America and the alternative of *tatting*

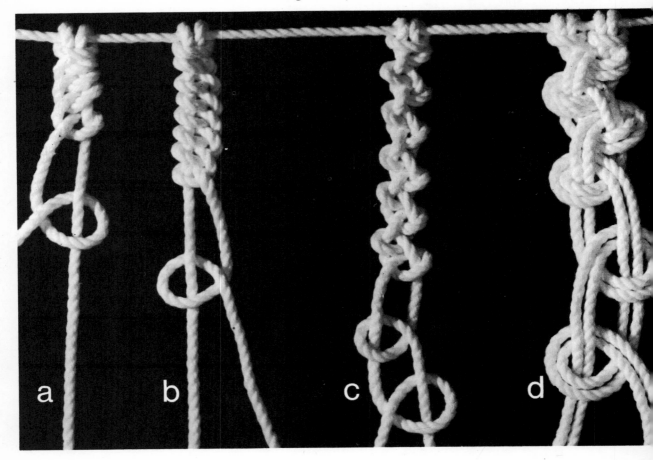

a b c d

knot is sometimes used by sailors. It can be worked from right or from left. To work from the left, hold the right-hand thread taut in the right hand and bring the left-hand thread up and over from front to back, pulling the end through the loop formed. To work from the right, hold the left-hand thread taut and make the half hitch with the right-hand thread.

Simple knots worked alternately from left and right make a *chain*. The chain can be worked with either single or double threads (figure 36c and d). Chains are sometimes referred to by sailors as *see-saw knots*.

The simple knot or half-hitch also forms the basis of *cording*, one of the most important processes in macramé work. Cording consists of *double* half-hitches worked

36 *Opposite   Left to right*   Simple knot worked from the left; simple knot worked from the right; single chain; double chain

37   Horizontal cording, stages one and two

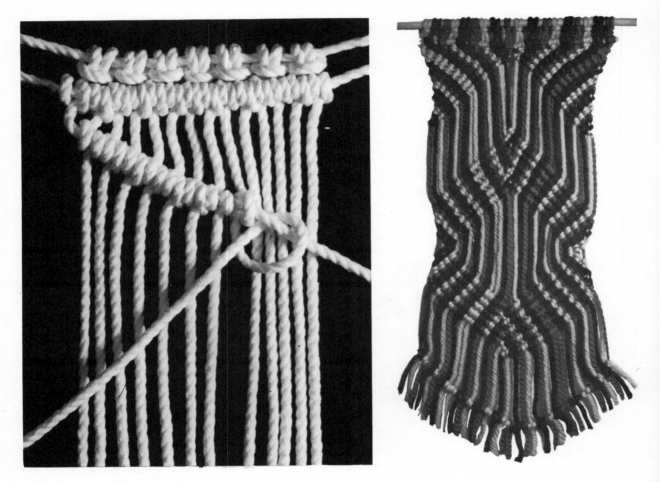

38 *Left* Cording on the oblique.
The leader is held at an angle of 45°

39 *Right* Small multi-coloured rug
wool hanging in cording. Made by
Carol Outram at Hornsey College of
Art

over a foundation cord. This cord is known as a *leader* and may, in different circumstances be horizontal, vertical or diagonal.

It is usual to work a row of horizontal cording immediately after setting on threads, as this gives a firm foundation to the work. A separate leader may be attached at the top left, or the left-hand warp may be used.

To work cording from left to right hold the leader taut in the right hand in a horizontal position. Starting from the left, bring up each warp thread in turn and wrap *twice* round the leader (ie, making two half-hitches) (figure 37). To work from the right, hold the leader (the right-hand thread) in the left hand and make the double half-hitches from right to left with each warp thread in turn. For diagonal cording, hold the leader at an angle of 45° and proceed as above (figure 38).

Rows of cording can be worked close together to form solid fabrics, or they can be spaced out and alternated with other knots or beads (figures 50 and 79).

The other important knot in macramé work is the *flat knot*, which is, in effect, a *reef knot* tied over a central core. It is often called *Solomon's knot* and, by sailors, *square knot*. Indeed, in the navy, macramé is more usually termed square knotting because of the predominance of this knot in the work.

The flat knot is usually worked on a group of four threads, the two central threads acting as a core (sometimes known as a *filler cord*). Knotting is made easier if the centre threads are kept taut and this can be done in several different ways; (*a*) with the fingers (figure 42); (*b*) by tucking the ends into the worker's belt; (*c*) if one is working on a board or frame, by fixing some attach-

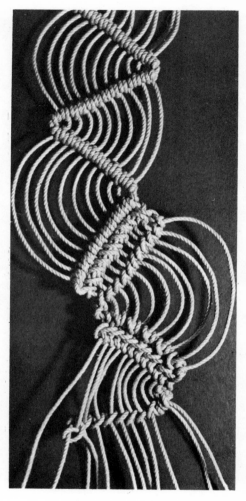

40 Experimental cording by Michael Halsey

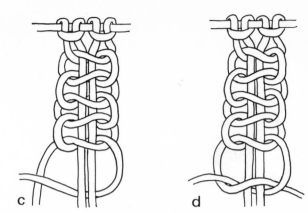

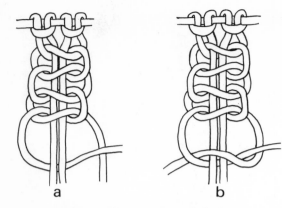

41   *a* and *b*, half knot   *c* and *d*, the
completed flat knot

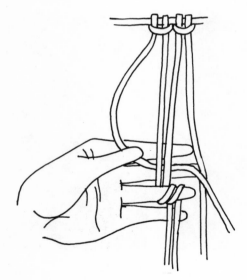

42   Holding the threads for a flat
knot

ment to the end of the board nearest the worker, to
which the ends could be tied, say a screw ring raised
slightly on a small wooden block or a G-clamp. The
threads must be raised enough for the fingers to mani-
pulate the knots easily.

To work a flat knot on four threads (*a*) pass the left
thread under the centre warp threads and over the right-
hand thread to form a loop (figure 41a); (*b*) pick up the
end of the right-hand thread and pass it from front to
back through the loop (figure 41b). Draw up tightly.
You have now made a *half knot* or *macramé knot*. (*c*)
Pass the right-hand thread under the centre threads and
over the left-hand thread (the reverse of (*a*)) (figure
41c); (*d*) put the end of the left-hand thread through the
loop from front to back. Draw up tightly (figure 41d).
The flat knot is now complete.

A flat knot repeated on the same threads, forms a
Solomon's bar (figure 72a) which can be used as braid
for trimming, or, in a suitable thread for a narrow belt,
dog lead, or bag handle. For variations on Solomon's
bar see figure 72b, c, and d.

38

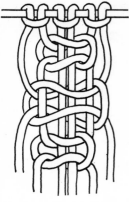

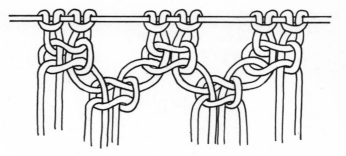

A *triple knot* consists of a flat knot plus a half knot.

Flat knot on six threads. (a) With the four centre threads work a normal flat knot. (b) Using these four threads as a centre core, tie the left- and right-hand threads into a flat knot. (c) as (a), (figure 43).

Making a fabric (figure 44)

To make a fabric, flat knots are alternated in the following way:

Set on threads in multiples of four.

First row on each group of four threads work a flat knot.

Second row leave the first two threads. With the next four threads (ie, two from the first knot in the row above, two from the second) work a flat knot. Continue to the end of the line, when there will be two threads left.

Third row as the first

Fourth row as the second

Repeat these four rows until the fabric reaches the required length.

Knotted in a stiff twine, the work gives the appearance of the traditional wine-glass pattern (figure 45).

43   *Left*   Flat knot on six threads

44   *Right*   Alternated flat knots

45   Alternated flat knots, worked in a stiff cord

46 Flat knot balls

47 Alternated flat knots in ribbon. Worked by Carol Outram

The same method can be used when working flat knots on six threads by taking *three* threads from each group in the second row.

Flat knot balls
Attractive three-dimensional balls can be worked with flat knots as follows.
(*a*) Work a number of flat knots. (*b*) Pick up the ends of the two centre threads and pass them from front to back through the work immediately above the first knot in the series. (*c*) Pull through until the last knot touches the first and forms the ball. The next flat knot worked holds the ball in place (figure 46).

A few other knots are incorporated into macramé and these are explained on the following pages.

Overhand knot (figure 51)   Also known as *thumb knot*, is simply a knot made in a single, double, or group of threads. When used as part of a design, it is sometimes referred to as a *shell knot* (figure 75d and figure 64).

48　Flat knots and cording, with china beads

49　Hanging in rugwool by Jane Smith, student at Stourbridge College of Art

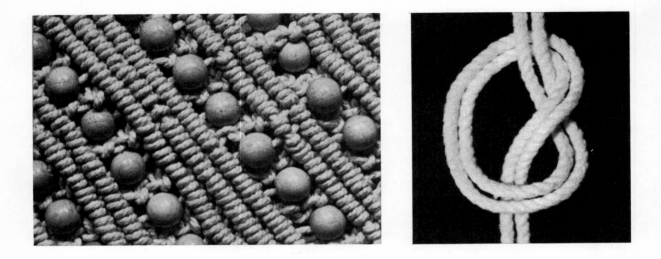

50 *Left* Cording in twine, with natural wood beads

51 *Right* Overhand knot

Marling knot This knot, often found on fringes on sailors' work, consists of an overhand knot (figure 51) made in one thread (or group of threads) over another at right angles to it (figure 52).

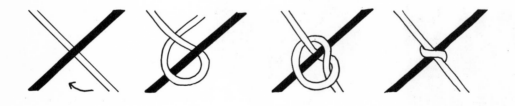

52 Marling knot, often found in nautical work

Turk's head The Turk's head can be used flat or as a ball. The working method is shown below (figure 53). When the first three loops have been formed, the thread follows the same journey again. Care must be taken to see that each thread goes over and under in exactly the same places as in the first looping. To convert this flat knot into a ball, the thread must be eased gradually along its length until the rounded shape is achieved.

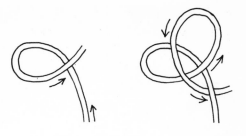

53   Method of working Turk's head

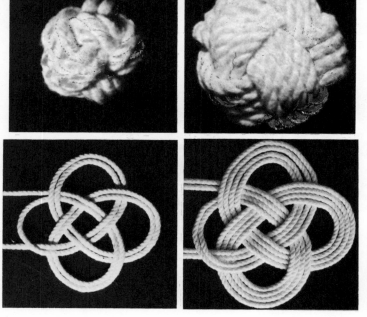

54   *Left*   Turk's head in single thread, (*above*) drawn up and (*below*) flat   *Right*   Turk's head in double thread, (*above*) drawn up and (*below*) flat

55 Three plaits

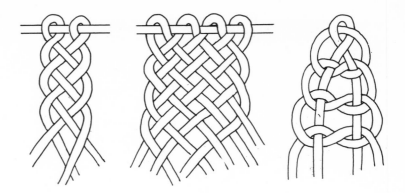

Plaiting of various kinds can be combined with macramé knots, and is useful for making a firm edge around an otherwise flimsy article.

56 Plaited wool border in browns and yellows by Michael Halsey

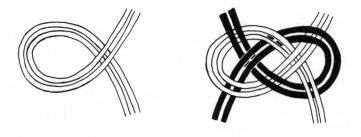

Josephine knot Also known as *Chinese knot* and *Carrick bend*. The josephine knot is worked with two threads or two groups of threads laid flat, in a simple over and under arrangement (figure 57). It is best worked on a flat, horizontal surface. An ironing board is ideal, as the threads can be pinned to facilitate working.

Japanese knot (figure 58) A more elaborate fancy knot, which, like the chinese knot, looks best worked from several threads laid side by side.

58 Japanese knot

45

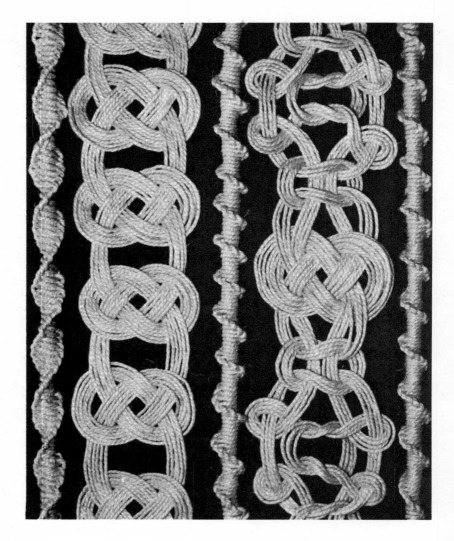

59   Detail of the three fold screen
worked in sisal, shown opposite

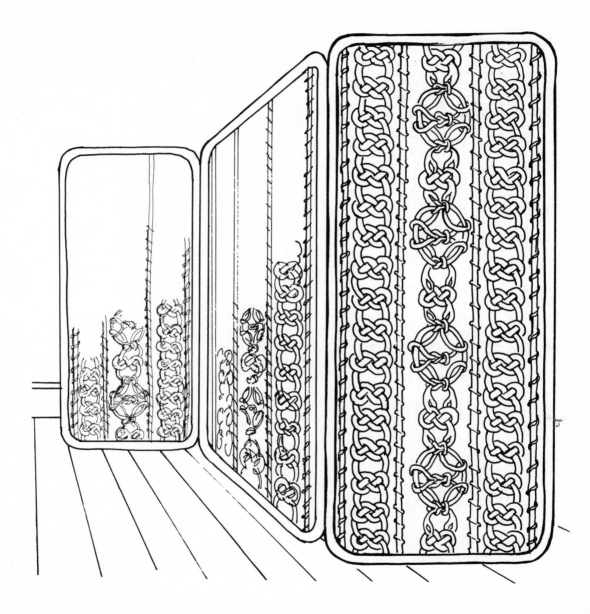

Fringes

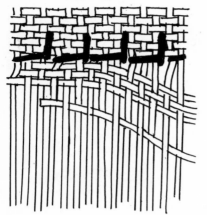

The fringe is probably the earliest form of macramé, being worked from the spare warp at either end of a piece of fabric when it was taken off the loom. When a fringe is knotted from the end of a piece of ready-made fabric, a row of hemstitching should be worked in the appropriate place and the weft threads withdrawn up to this point (figure 60). The hemstitching (figure 61) serves to neaten the edge of the fabric and to tie the warp threads into convenient bundles for knotting, most fabric threads being too fine to knot singly. When a tough canvas is used as in the sailors' fringe (figure 63) hemstitching is not necessary.

In later developments of macramé, fringes came to be worked independently of the fabric and attached after completion; for this kind of work the threads must be set on to a foundation thread, possibly with a fancy heading.

60   Withdrawing weft threads after working hemstitching

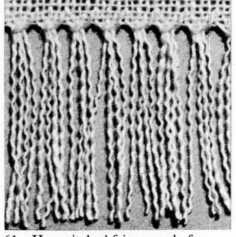

61   Hemstitched fringe ready for knotting

Plate 3   Opposite
Sisal rug in diagonal cording with fringe of josephine knots made by Janet Oliver

48

62 Lampshade with deep macramé
fringe and with single chains
emphasising the struts

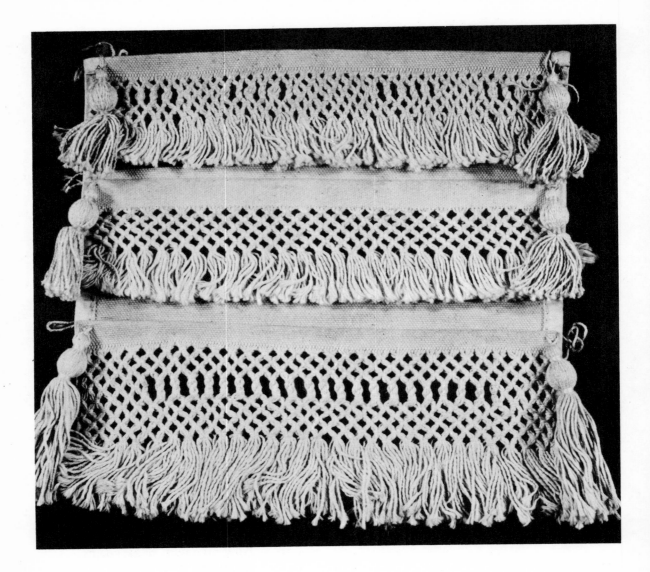

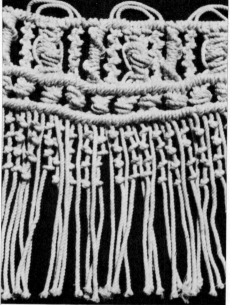

64 Fringed border, possibly sailors' work *From the collection of Valerie Cliffe*

65 Heavy fringe in white garden twine

63 *Opposite* Set of wall pockets with seized fringe and tassels Sailors' work *By courtesy of the National Maritime Museum, Greenwich*

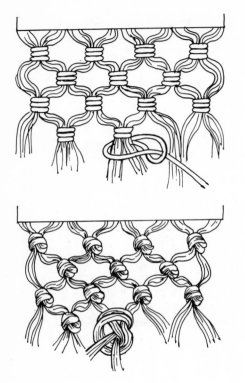

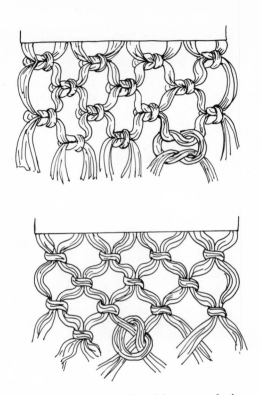

Four fringes found in sailors' work, either on their own or combined with more elaborate macramé work.

1 *Seized fringe*. This term refers to a fringe which is bound together by a separate thread, rather than by knotting the existing threads. It is used widely in nautical work. (*Above left* figure 66.)

2 *Reef knot*. Worked as for a flat knot but without the central core. (*Above right* figure 67.)

3 *Overhand knot*. Explained in figure 51. (*Below left* figure 68.)

4 *Marling knot*. See figure 52. (*Below right* figure 69.)

70 *Left* Two Victorian fringes, worked in Devon about a hundred years ago. The one below is a mantelpiece edging *Both from the collection of Miss Dorothy Holman*

71 *Above* Combination of macramé and plaiting, worked in multi-coloured garden twines

Braids

Braids serve as an excellent introduction to macramé. They are quick to work and have a wide variety of uses as trimmings on dress and in the home. In old pattern books braids are sometimes referred to as *galloons*, and in nautical work as *sennits* or *sinnets*. A very simple narrow braid can be made by working a series of flat knots and with slight modification to the basic knot, a number of variations can be achieved. Most braids have traditional names, and these have been used whenever possible. Most of the braids which are worked over a central core are termed bars.

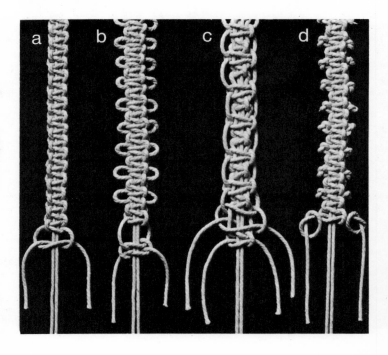

72 (*a*) Solomon's bar. A series of flat, or Solomon's knots
(*b*) Solomon's bar with picots. The picot is formed by completing the whole flat knot a little way down the centre core, drawing it up tightly and then pushing it up into place below the last knot. The picots can be spaced out as desired; for example, every second or third knot (*c*) Solomon's bar on six threads. The method for working a Solomon's knot on six threads is given in figure 43 (*d*) Solomon's bar with side knots. Between alternate flat knots, a small overhand knot is worked close to the last knot on both right and left hand thread

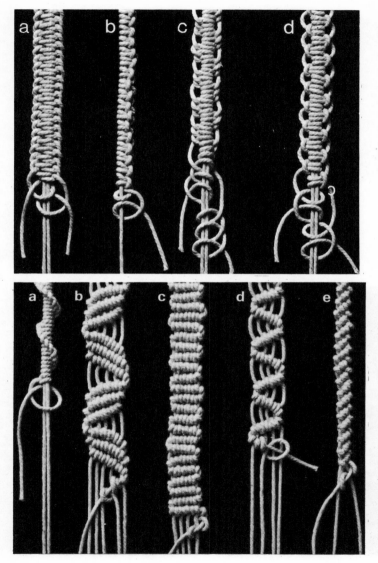

73 Braids based on simple knots (or half-hitches) (*a*) Single genoese bar. A simple knot worked alternately from right and left round the central warp threads (*b*) Single tatted bar. A half-hitch followed by a reverse half-hitch (*c*) Treble genoese bar. Groups of three half-hitches worked alternately from right and left (*d*) Tatted bar. A half-hitch followed by a reverse half-hitch as in (*a*) but worked from alternate sides

74 Braids based on half-hitches and cording (*a*) Corkscrew bar. A series of half-hitches worked from one side will form a spiral round the leader (*b*), (*c*), (*d*) and (*e*) are based on cording. As they have no core, they are not termed bars (*b*) for the ribs sloping down from left to right, the left hand thread is used each time as a leader. For those down from right to left, the right hand thread (*c*) and (*d*) one long leader is attached at the top left and is used continuously throughout, being held in the right or left hand as required. It is held horizontally for (*c*) and at 45° for (*d*) (*e*) the right hand thread is used as the leader for each row of cording

75 (*a*) Double chain. Simple knots worked from right and left alternately with double threads
(*b*) Bannister bar. A spiral made by working the *first half only* of a flat knot in series   (*c*) Waved bar. Groups of seven half-hitches alternated from side to side
(*d*) Solomon's bar with shell knot. The shell knots which are alternated with the flat knots are merely overhand knots made in the centre core

76 *Below left* Two more elaborate braids, worked in twine

77 *Below right* Wide braid in cording, flat knots and chains

The simplest and most commonly found fabrics in macramé are made of alternated flat knots and their many variations. Diagonal cording, on its own or combined with other knots is also versatile. Any border pattern can be adapted to a fabric by working several borders side by side down from the same foundation thread and linking across as often as is necessary for the strength of the fabric. Most fabrics are strong enough to stand up to wear on their own, but can be mounted on to a woven fabric for extra strength. This was done on

Fabrics

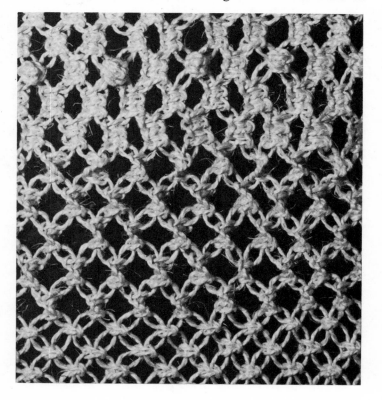

78   Sampler of variations on alternated flat knots

the evening coat in colour plates 4a and b, made entirely of josephine knots in wool, which would otherwise have sagged.

When making a fabric it is advisable to work one motif of the design to ascertain the scale and number of threads required. Warp threads can then be set on in the appropriate multiple of this number to produce the desired width of fabric. Bags, skirts, etc, can be made in a tubular fashion, thus doing away with the need for side seams.

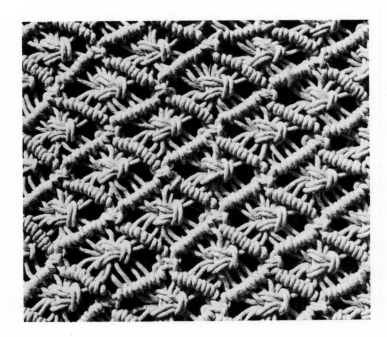

79 Fabric based on diagonal cording with flat knots

A garment such as a jacket or top, is best worked over a simple paper pattern, and can be knotted from the neck downwards or from the bottom up.

The jacket in figure 82 was worked from the top down in the following way:

A long chain was crocheted and tacked round the outline of the jacket pattern from the bottom of one side seam, up over the shoulders and neck down the opposite side, but not along the bottom of the garment. The knotting threads were then set on into the chain along the shoulders and neck, and the knotting begun. At both ends of each row, the threads were attached to the chain (figure 80). Increasing for the arm-hole was done by adding new threads where necessary (figure 84) and the work continued to the bottom where the ends were

Making up garments

80 *Below left* Attaching the knots to a crocheted chain outline

81 *Below right* Detail of a jacket made from rouleau strips in a printed fabric to match a dress. The jacket is edged with a border of plaiting. Designed and made by Cassandra Mayne

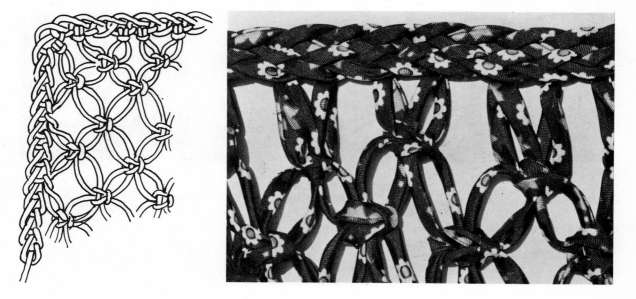

82 Jacket in white vest cotton, with silver papier mâché beads. Designed and made at Hornsey College of Art by Janet Oliver

left in a fringe. Washable papier mâché beads were inserted between the knots in parts of the design. Each part of the jacket and the sleeves were treated in this way. When the knotting was complete the chain gave a firm edging and the pieces could be overcast or crocheted together, giving neat seams.

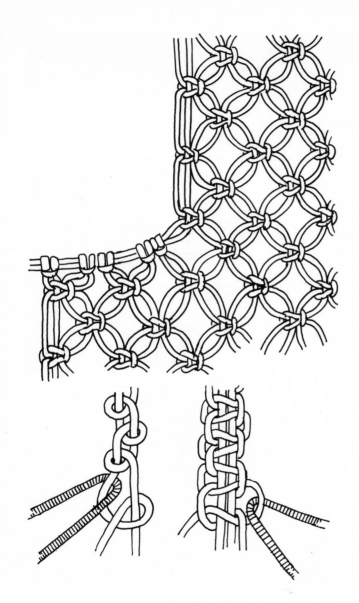

83 Shaping for the armhole when working from the top

84 Increasing.
Left into chains; *right* into flat knots

85 Shaping from armhole when working from the bottom of the garment

When starting from the bottom of the garment, the threads can be set on with picots, giving a decorative edge. The armhole can be shaped simply by leaving knots on the outer edge. Later the ends can be cut and darned in. All edges should be bound before assembling the garment (figure 85).

If the macramé is mounted on to a fabric, all seams can be machined in the normal way.

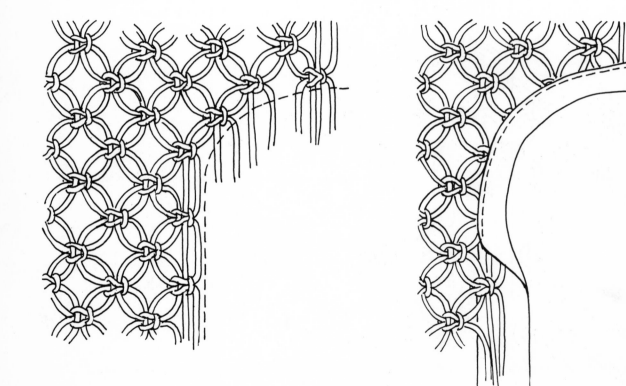

Six bags

86　Evening bag in fine pink thread.
Worked by Margaret Gains at Wall
Hall College of Education

87   Handbag on sale in Greece today
*From the collection of Marianne
Straub*

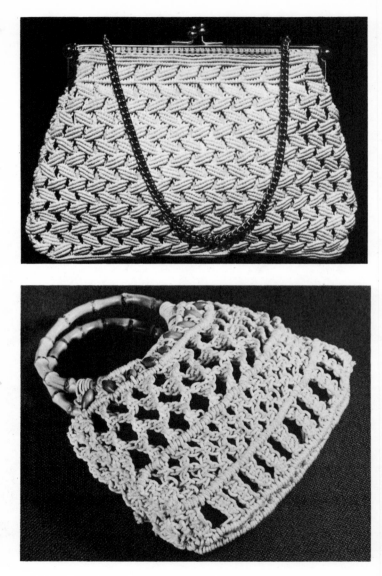

88   Handbag worked by Jenny
Lund, a first year student at Bath
College of Home Economics

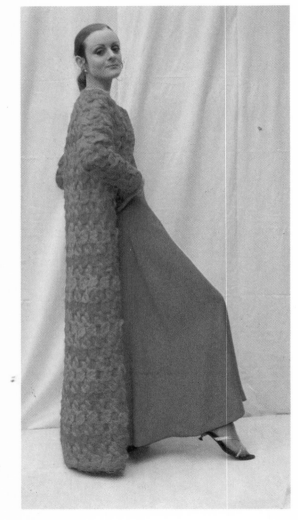
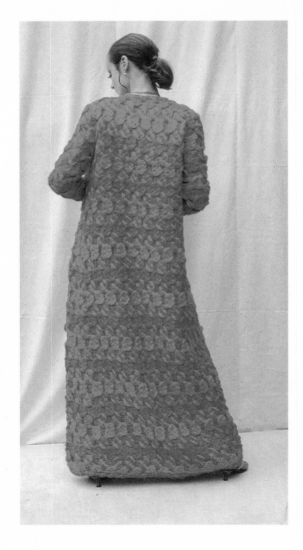

Plate 4
Evening coat in wool, worked entirely in josephine knots mounted over taffeta. Designed and made by Judith Stone at Hornsey College of Art

89 Bag by Ellyn Elson, a first year student at Bath College of Home Economics

90 Bucket bag in red leather with macramé inset. Worked by Hilda Roe at Wall Hall College of Education

91 Modern Turkish shopping bag on sale commercially *From the collection of Marianne Straub*

66

1 The macramé may be in the form of a panel set in to a leather bag (figure 90).

2 Mounted over fabric, a macramé bag could be made up in to an envelope shape (figure 86).

3 Figure 94 shows a method used on commercially sold shopping bags. The ends are slipped through the ring on the handle, doubled back and bound, then trimmed to a convenient length on the inside of the bag.

4 Solomon's bars can be set directly on to a string handle (figure 95). The main body of the bag is worked in alternating flat knots (figure 44).

Making up bags

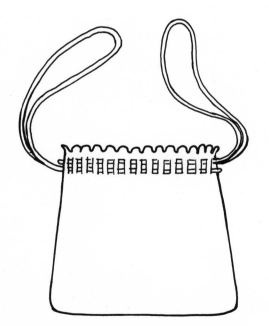

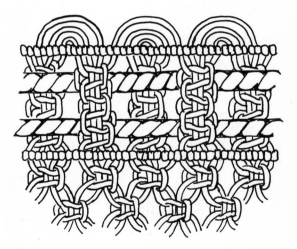

92 Drawstring bag, with detail (*right*) of top showing Solomon's bars through which drawstring is threaded

5 Setting on to a wooden or plastic handle and working downwards (figures 93a and c). The knots can be linked laterally to form a cylinder, doing away with the necessity for side seams. At the bottom, the ends are knotted together on the inside and trimmed, or on the outside, to form a decorative fringe.

6 The ends can be set directly on to a wooden or leather base and worked upwards (figure 93b). The top could be finished with a border of detached Solomon's bars through which a drawstring is threaded (figure 92).

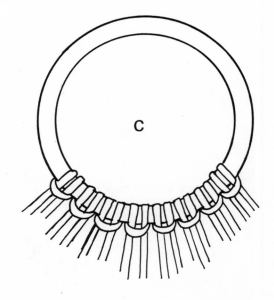

93 Three ways of setting on threads for a bag

94 Handle of a shopping bag from Communist China

95 Detail of bag in figure 91, showing method of setting on threads

Shoes

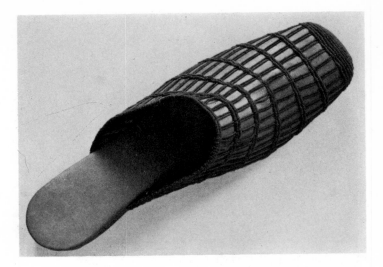

96 Mule worked in cording, mounted over a fabric. Made by Janet Oliver at Hornsey College of Art

97 White shoe with macramé inset. Made by Janet Oliver

It is obviously impossible to make up proper shoes at home. However, slippers, beach and party shoes can be made fairly simply. The entire sole can be worked in cording and the ends of some of the leaders brought up and knotted into straps for instep and heel (figure 98b), or threads can be set directly into the perforated holes round a bought sole (as in the handbag base in figure 93b).

The barefoot party sandal in figure 98a has no sole, but merely slips over the second toe.

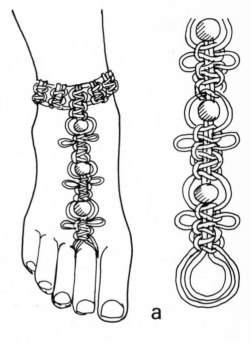

a

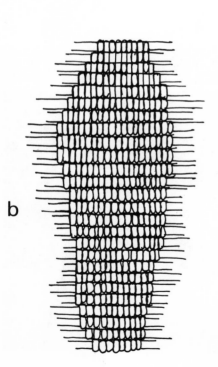

b

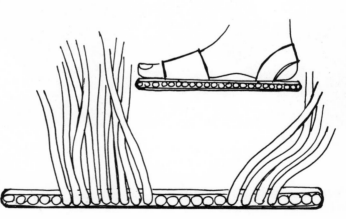

Belts

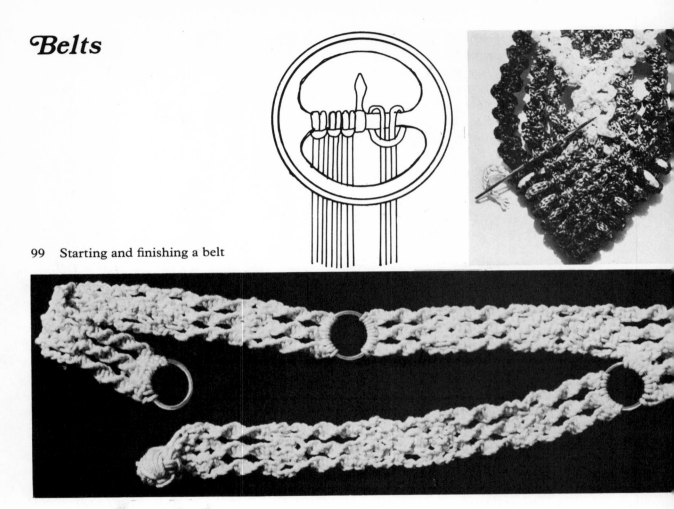

99   Starting and finishing a belt

100   Belt made by Joanna Thomas, aged twelve, in white piping cord on chromium rings. The belt is finished in a Turk's head which slips through the ring on the other end

101 Four belts *Left to right* Red
and white tubular synthetic cord;
black parcel string; beige, cream and
black tubular synthetic cord; black
plastic. The two black belts were
worked by Ann Mary Pilcher

Accessories

102 *Opposite left* Tie worked in knitting wool in five colours. Cording and flat knots are used

103 *Opposite right* Necklace in plastic covered twine with wooden beads

104 *Above* Collar in gold fingering by Dorothy Phillips, third year student at Bath College of Home Economics

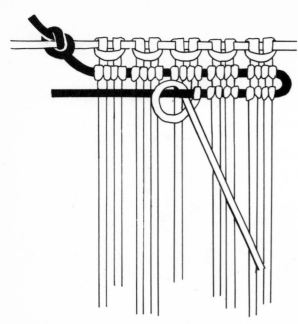

105   Horizontal and vertical cording
in Cavandoli work

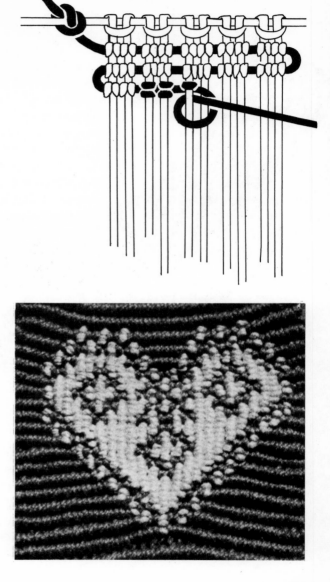

106   Heart motif in Cavandoli work

When macramé is worked in monochrome, the interest lies in the rich surface textures of the knots, but when the work is done in multicolours, the texture becomes subsidiary to the pattern made by the colours and tones. Whereas work in one colour needs a variety of knots to enrich the surface, macramé in two or more colours can look effective worked in one knot throughout.

A type of two-colour work, known as *Cavandoli* work, after Madame Cavandoli who taught it to children in Italy, is based simply on cording and makes a close, extremely hardwearing fabric. The principle is simple. Warp threads are set on in one colour *A* and a ball of thread in a contrasting colour *B* is attached at the top left hand corner of the work. This acts as the leader for horizontal cording. Naturally, it will be completely concealed and the knots will all appear in one colour *A*. When a knot in colour *B* is required the next *warp* thread is used as a leader and the cording worked over it vertically in colour *B*. Thus all the knots worked horizontally will appear in colour *A* and all those worked vertically in colour *B*.

Designs for Cavandoli work can be prepared on squared paper, each square representing a knot. Geometric motifs are suitable, also stylised plant, bird and animal forms, as used in cross stitch or canvas work. Because of the nature of the knot, designs become slightly elongated vertically in the working, and this must be allowed for in the preparation of the design.

When working in colour it is important to consider the relative tones of the threads used: (ie, how light or dark they are, irrespective of their actual *hue*). The pattern in figure 109 would lose all its point if the tones did not shade from light to dark.

Colour

107   Initial E in Cavandoli work

108 *Left* Part of a wool hanging with wooden beads by Carol Outram, student at Hornsey College of Art

109 *Right* Wide braid in tubular synthetic cord in three shades of beige, cream and black

Work in multicolour needs careful planning on paper, or by means of trial samplers. The problem of making a colour 'travel' from one part of the design to another is a fascinating one. Cording in particular is useful, since any thread used as a leader is concealed entirely and can reappear where needed in the design.

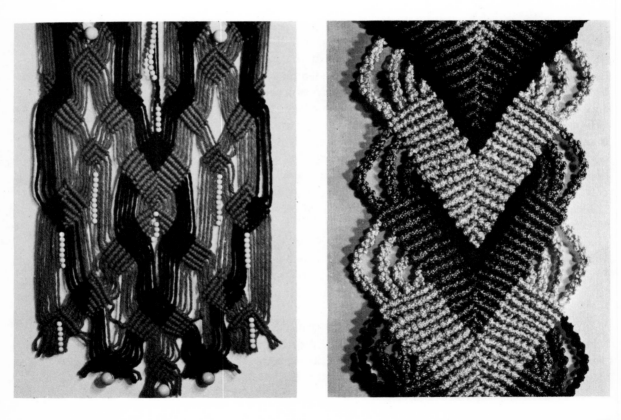

Free use of Macramé

110   Hanging by Althea Hill,
student at Bath College of Home
Economics. In greys purples and
yellows, the design was the result of
studying the façades of slum
buildings during a college project.
Rug wool, jute string and cotton cord
are used

111   A set of models from 127 mm
to 228 mm (5 in. to 9 in.) in height,
by Sheila Sharp, post graduate
student at Birmingham College of
Art

112   *Opposite*   One of the designs
on this page enlarged to 1525 mm
(5 ft) and carried out in white cotton
yachting rope, by Sheila Sharp

In the past, macramé has been used mainly for the making of useful articles, and designs have tended to remain formal and geometric in character. There is no reason however, why knotting should not be used in a completely 'free' way.

When one can dispense with the purely practical considerations of strength, washability and wearing qualities, a far wider range of threads can be used. Also, the mixing of different types of thread in one piece of work, and the introduction of paper or raffia beads, for example, is feasible. Knots need not be worked regularly (colour plate 1 *Mexican Sun*) and lengths of thread may be left without any knots at all (figures 110, 112, 116 and colour plate 2).

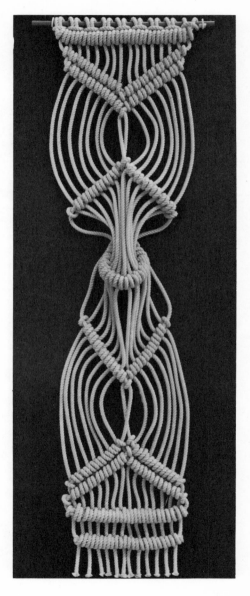

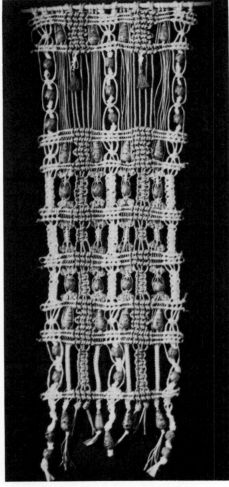

113 *Left* Hanging by Ann Croot
114 *Right* Detail of panel
showing twine, beads, nylon
and cellophane threads

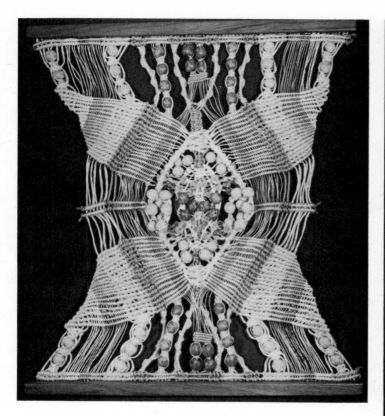

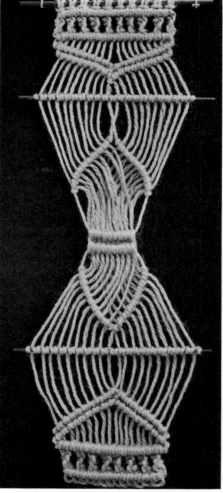

115 *Left* *Flower* by Ann Croot
116 *Right* Large hanging in sisal, by Sheila Sharp

There is room too, for experiment with three-dimensional work such as knotting on to wire constructions, making mobiles, etc. (figures 122, 123 and 124).

The panels opposite are the results of an experiment by the author to use macramé for figurative work. In the head (figure 118), the face is worked entirely in cording. Off-white knitting wool was set on along the top, then appropriately coloured threads were positioned on a vertical foundation cord down the left hand side. White areas were then worked in horizontal cording, and coloured areas in vertical cording, on much the same principle as Cavandoli work (figure 105). The hair was very freely knotted and the whole mounted on to a fabric base.

The tree (figure 117) is also very free in treatment with beads incorporated into the knots, and a mixture of knitting wools (some textured) used. The trunk is in cording and the river in a combination of cording and overhand knots with some areas left unknotted.

The panels are not entirely successful, being 'feelers' along new trains of thought on macramé, but with experience and consequent greater control, interesting figurative work could be done.

117 *Tree by the River* by Eirian Short. An attempt to use macramé for figurative work

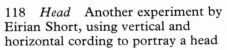

118 *Head* Another experiment by Eirian Short, using vertical and horizontal cording to portray a head

119   Detail of hanging worked by
Marion Smith Ferri in rug wools,
cotton rayon rug yarn and spun
rayon

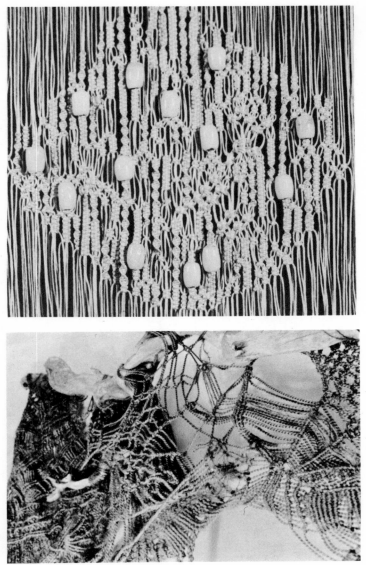

120   *Moon Flight – Apollo* 10
Detail of panel worked by Marion
Smith Ferri (USA). White linen and
opaque beads from India

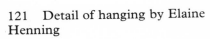

121   Detail of hanging by Elaine
Henning

122–4 Three dimensional macramé
by George Pfiffner

122 *Spire*

123 *Head*

124 *Torso*

Suppliers

In both Great Britain and in the United States of America good stationers, garden suppliers, hardware stores, yachting and marine suppliers, sell a variety of strings and ropes. Needlecraft as well as sewing departments of large stores stock threads of all kinds.

Below is a list of specialist suppliers in Great Britain who sell to the general public.

For all kinds of ropes, strings, nylon cords, fine twines, etc.

M. Mallock and Sons, 44 Vauxhall Bridge Road, London sw1

Arthur Beale, 194 Shaftesbury Avenue, London wc2
(Both sell over the counter to the general public and will sell small quantities.)

British Twines Ltd, 112 Green Lanes, London n16
(For schools or colleges who order in quantity, British Twines will dye strings to specification. Also, there are at times oddments of coloured strings at the factory, which they will sell off.)

Dryad Ltd, Northgates, Leicester, lei 4or
(Dryads sell a fine natural macramé twine in half-pound balls, but will only accept orders by post of the minimum value of £2.)

For piping cord

(In boxes, containing 23 m (25 yards) of the thickest cord to 274 m (300 yards) of the finest: bought this way, piping cord works out very economically.)

McCulloch and Wallis Ltd, 25-26 Dering Street, London w1

For rug wools, knitting wools, embroidery threads, nylon cords, synthetic metal threads, etc.

The Needlewoman Shop, 146-148 Regent Street, London w1

For beads

Ells and Farrier Ltd, 5 Princes Street, London w1

Bourne and Hollingsworth Ltd, Oxford Street, London w1

The Bead Shop, 53 South Molton Street, London w1

Bibliography

Macramé the Art of Creative Knotting   VIRGINIA I. HARVEY
Reinhold, New York 1967

Anchor Manual of Needlework   J. AND P. COATS   Batsford
1958 Third edition 1968 (One chapter on *Macramé*, one on
Cavandoli Work)

Encyclopaedia of Needlework   THÉRÈSE DE DILLMONT
Dillmont, Mulhouse, France: Toggitt, New York
(A nineteenth century book, which includes a
comprehensive chapter on *Macramé* now re-published in
facsimile and is distributed by C. and F. Handicraft
Supply Limited, 346 Stag Lane, Kingsbury, London w9)

Le Macramé   THÉRÈSE DE DILLMONT   From the D.M.C.
Library
(Secondhand copies may still be found)

The Ashley Book of Knots   CLIFFORD ASHLEY   Doubleday
1944

Designing with String   MARY SEYD   Batsford, London:
Watson-Guptill, New York

Creative Textile Design   ROLF HARTUNG   Batsford,
London: Reinhold, New York

Numerals in *italics* refer to figure numbers

Index

Note for American readers

Throughout read

Yarn for wool
Thread for cotton
Thumbtack for drawing pin
Clamp for bulldog clip
Thin wooden strip for batten
Braiding for plaiting
Straight pins for milliners' pins
Marine suppliers for ships' chandler
Basted for tacked

Printed in the United States of America
by the Halliday Lithograph Corporation
West Hanover, Massachusetts